Intensive Reading Course on Chinese Culture: Traditional Culture

中国文化精读教程：传统文化

冯薇薇 张超 编著

SinolinguA
华语教学出版社

First Edition 2025

ISBN 978-7-5138-2562-7

Published by Sinolingua Co., Ltd
24 Baiwanzhuang Street, Beijing 100037, China
Tel: (86)10-68320585, 68997826
Fax: (86)10-68997826, 68326333
http://www.sinolingua.com.cn
E-mail: hyjx@sinolingua.com.cn
Facebook: www.facebook.com/sinolingua
Printed by Beijing Hucais Culture Communication Co., Ltd

Printed in the People's Republic of China

前言

《中国文化精读教程》是参照《国际中文教育中文水平等级标准》和《国际中文教育用中国文化和国情教学参考框架》（简称《参考框架》）的指导和要求开发而成的系列教程。本系列教程语言难度控制在《国际中文教育中文水平等级标准》中级的水平，文化理解的分级目标控制在《参考框架》中级阶段，可应用于海外各个国家中学到大学阶段，亦可与国际中文教育精读课程（中级）相结合。

本系列教程共三册，每个分册分别对应《参考框架》中级阶段的三大主题——社会生活、传统文化和当代中国，涵盖15个话题，设置30篇课文，覆盖80多个文化点，力求完成中级阶段所要求的教学内容和目标，即：了解中国社会生活、传统文化和当代中国国情的基本知识，比较中国文化和本土文化的主要异同，理解多样性。每篇课文的教学内容包括：课文阅读（附英文翻译）、短视频、生词表、语法点、结构分析、练习、文化教学活动。课文的词汇难度控制在4～6级之间，每篇课文包含约20个生词，3～5个成语或惯用语，1～3个语法点。

本系列教程选材兼具趣味性和讨论性。我们精心挑选了一系列文化趣事、社科美文、热点新闻，以及爆款视频的文本，确保课程内容丰富多元、动态活泼，力求在体现中华文化深厚底蕴的同时也能反映当下中国社会的热点话题。我们希望这些文章能够引领学生深入探索中国文化的内涵，发现文化差异，拓展视野，激发学生对中华文化和跨文化交际的热情与好奇心。本系列教程中还设计了丰富的文化探究活动和课堂讨论环节，旨在从多个角度、多个层面引导学生探索文化的奥秘，启发学生思考。

我们希望，通过学习本系列教程，学生不仅能够深入了解中华文化，更能够提升跨文化交际敏感度和能力，成为真正具有国际视野的人才。

目录

话题一 历史

教学内容和目标	文化点
1. 了解中国标志性的历史事件及其历史意义。 2. 理解中国历史进程和历史事件对现代中国的意义和影响。	古代史，现代史，汉唐盛世，明朝郑和下西洋

故宫博物院

课文 1　北京中轴线

课前热身

请仔细观察下面这张图片，用两分钟左右的时间描述一下你在图片上看到了什么，以及你对图片的理解。

课文 1

扫一扫，看视频

北京中轴线

从永定门到钟鼓楼、贯穿紫禁城南北、全长近 8 公里的中轴线是古都北京的中心标志，也是世界上现存最长的城市中轴线。“中轴突出、两翼对称”是北京城市格局的最大特色。

北京的中轴线历史可以追溯到距今 700 多年的元朝，元世祖忽必烈放弃旧都城，在其东北方择址建设元朝新国都——元大都（即现在的北京），那时的中轴线长 3.7 公里。后经明清时期发展至今，北京的中轴线延长至 7.86 公里。

“择天下之中而立国，择国之中而立宫”。这是中国古代建都城的核心思想。这里的“国”指国都，“中”代表中心。紫禁城坐落于中轴线的中心位置，由皇城、内城、外城层层相套防卫，皇宫内最高等级的宫殿和城门直接建在中轴线上，犹如居“天下之中”，既显示出皇权至高无上的威严，又把帝都北京统领成了一个不可分割的整体。围绕古都中轴线对称布局是古代北京城市规划建筑与封建社会的政治、文化观念的有机统一。中轴线北边和南边为商业区，沿中轴线两侧则为百姓的生活和休闲区。

中轴线是一座城的脊梁，它展现出的严谨、对称与秩序体现了“以中为尊”的价值观及“天人合一”的信仰，是传统哲学思想在城市建设上的反映，也蕴含着中国人的为人处世之道。

中轴线汇集了北京古代建筑的精髓，见证了北京城的沧桑变迁。建筑大师梁思成曾写道：“北京独有的壮美秩序就由这条中轴的建立而产生……气魄之雄伟就在这个南北延伸、一贯到底的规模。”

如今，北京中轴线仍具有旺盛的生命力和历史纵深感。在北京新的规划蓝图中，这一令世人赞叹的城市景观再次向南北两侧延伸，连接北起奥林匹克公园、南至南五环外的广阔地区，成为集中体现古都保护和城市发展的一条新轴线。

2012 年，北京中轴线被列入《中国世界文化遗产预备名单》。2021 年，北京中轴线申遗文本编写完成，并通过联合国教科文组织世界遗产中心的格式审查，申遗工作进入关键时期，力争在 2035 年申遗成功。中轴线这个古老的北京符号将焕发出它更加生机勃勃的魅力。

The Central Axis of Beijing

The Central Axis of Beijing, stretching nearly eight km from Yongding Gate in the south to the Bell Tower in the north, is the core area of the old city of Beijing. It is also the longest urban central axis still existing in the world. With its symbolic importance, the Central Axis of Beijing divides the city into two symmetric wings. The central axis is the symbol of Beijing's urban spatial pattern.

The Central Axis of Beijing has its roots dating back to the Yuan

Dynasty (1206-1368). Kublai Khan, also known as Shizu Emperor of the Yuan Dynasty, jettisoned the old capital city of Zhongdu and built the new capital city of Dadu (present Beijing) in its northeast. The Central Axis of Beijing was 3.7 km in length at that time. With further development in the Ming and Qing dynasties, it was at last extended to 7.86 km.

What influenced traditional Chinese capital planning was a fundamental principle that people should build a country at the center of the world and construct the royal palace at the center of the country. The Forbidden City, built along the Central Axis of Beijing, has a group of royal palaces surrounded and protected by the inner and outer courts. Influenced by the architectural philosophy of "sitting at the center of the world", the Chinese built the most high-ranking royal palaces and city gates in the Forbidden City. As a symbol of the supreme authority of the emperor, the Central Axis also links and integrates the different parts of Beijing. Its symmetrical pattern embodies an urban planning principle and ancient Chinese society's political and cultural ideologies. Areas to the north and south of the Central Axis were urban business districts and those on the two sides of it were for residential and recreational purposes.

The central axis is the backbone of a city. With its preference for precision, symmetry, and orderliness, the Central Axis of Beijing epitomizes the "value of the center" in Chinese culture. It highlights the Chinese belief in the harmony between nature and humans. It is a typical example of traditional Chinese philosophy applied to urban planning and embodies the Chinese way of socialization.

Most of the iconic buildings in the old city of Beijing are along the Central Axis, which witnessed the evolution and changes of this city. Liang Sicheng, a renowned Chinese architect, wrote, "Beijing's splendor and orderliness come from this central axis. It extends to both the north and south, imposing a sense of magnificence on the whole city".

Today, the Central Axis of Beijing is still in full vigor and of historical significance. In Beijing's new urban planning blueprint, this spectacular urban landscape will extend further to both the north and south. It will link the Olympic Park in the north with the vast land outside of the Fifth Ring Road in the south. In the future, it will become a new axis that witnesses the conservation of the old city and the development of new Beijing.

In 2012, the Central Axis of Beijing was included on the preliminary list of China's world cultural heritage sites. In 2021, the application text was completed and passed the format review of the UNESCO World Heritage Center. The application work has entered a crucial stage, which is expected to be completed by 2035. As a landmark of this old city, the Central Axis of Beijing is set to retain its charm and vitality.

生词表

生词

1. 中轴线	zhōngzhóuxiàn	Central Axis
2. 贯穿	guànchuān	run through

练习

1. 根据课文内容回答下面的问题。（5 分）

（1）北京的中轴线是什么走向的？（1 分）

（2）北京的城市格局有什么特点？（2 分）

（3）元朝的时候，中轴线的长度是多少？（1 分）

（4）紫禁城与中轴线有什么关系？（1 分）

2. 请在课文中找出与下面解释对应的词语。（5 分）

（1）基本原则或主要理念 ________________

（2）形容地位最高，没有能超过的 ________________

（3）不容许割裂、拆开 ________________

（4）做人和对待事情的方式 ________________

（5）形容生命力旺盛，富有活力 ________________

3. 根据课文内容判断下面说法的对错，并说明理由（5 分）

	对	错
（1）从永定门到钟鼓楼的北京中轴线全长超过 8 公里。	□	□
理由：____		
（2）“择天下之中而立国，择国之中而立宫”里的“中”代表中国。	□	□
理由：____		
（3）中轴线只有最南边是商业区。	□	□
理由：____		
（4）梁思成见证了北京城的沧桑变迁。	□	□
理由：____		
（5）现在，中轴线的北端以奥林匹克公园为起点。	□	□
理由：____		

课文 2　千年大运河

课前热身

请仔细观察下面这张图片，用两分钟左右的时间描述一下你在图片上看到了什么，以及你对图片的理解。

课文 2

扫一扫，看视频

千年大运河

在中国的中东部平原有一条蜿蜒千里的大运河，它的修建开通推进了中国古代的经济发展和社会变革，见证了无数个时代的更迭。大运河是流淌了千年的水上文明，是一部书写在华夏大地上的宏伟诗篇。

大运河，由京杭大运河、隋唐大运河、浙东运河组成，跨越北京、天津、河北、山东、河南、安徽、江苏、浙江八省（市），连通海河、黄河、淮河、长江和钱塘江五大水系，全长近3200公里。

大运河的开凿始于春秋时期，完成于隋代，繁荣于唐宋。大运河的开通打通了南北水上交通的大动脉。南北方贸易往来日益增多，文化、思想、观念、艺术等精神领域的交流亦不断延伸扩展。北方大漠孤烟的豪爽与南方小桥流水的柔和在运河之上相互交融，彼此影响，运河文化带由此繁盛起来。2500年的岁月中，它的宽阔与包容连通了南方与北方，也串起了繁荣与生机，成就了沿岸一个又一个富足的城市。

大运河深深地影响了老百姓的日常生活。源源不绝的运河水滋养了运河两岸的人们，灌溉农田，便利水运，运河边码头、城镇、集市、商铺、手工作坊逐渐兴起，沿岸的盐业、茶业、丝织业等蓬勃发展，运河上船舶往来，商贾云集，熙熙攘攘，好一派繁荣热闹的景象。正是这运河中灵动的水，衍生出了运河两岸丰富的地域文化、水利文化、船舶文化、商贾文化，以及丰富的民间艺术、精湛的手工技艺、深厚的传统习俗，运河沿岸文化千百年来一直散发着勃勃生机。

大运河记录了中国历史文化的壮美和辉煌，见证了中华文明的源远流长和中华民族的勤劳智慧。如今，随着“一带一路”合作倡议、长江经济带发展计划的提出，大运河迎来新的机遇。中国政府颁布了《大运河文化保护传承利用规划纲要》，对大运河的保护做出规划，分析现存的难题，挖掘大运河优秀传统文化精神内涵，在文化遗产保护、生态发展、河道水系治理、非遗传承、文化旅游等方面做出新的努力与尝试，形成区域发展的新模式，让大运河文化“活”起来、“火”起来。

运河不能只有沧桑的回忆，更要有光辉的未来。中国人民将始终怀着敬畏历史之心，在新时代继续延续壮美运河的千年神韵，让运河文化之水、生态之水长流不止，生生不息。

The Grand Canal

On the central-eastern plains of China, there is a winding Grand Canal. It shaped the economic and social development of ancient China and witnessed the changing eras. The Grand Canal, a water civilization which has been flowing for millenniums, is regarded as a great poem written on the land of China.

The Grand Canal is composed of the Beijing-Hangzhou Grand Canal, the Sui and Tang Grand Canal, and the East Zhejiang Canal. With a total length of nearly 3,200 kilometers, it stretches along eight provinces and cities, including Beijing, Tianjin, Hebei, Shandong, Henan, Anhui, Jiangsu, and Zhejiang. It connects the Haihe River, Yellow River, Huaihe River, Yangtze River, and Qiantang River.

The construction of the Grand Canal began in the Spring and Autumn Period (770-476 BC) and was completed in the Sui Dynasty (581-618). The Tang (618-907) and Song (960-1279) dynasties was a golden era of its development. The Grand Canal opened up the main artery of the north-south water communication. Trade along its route was booming, and exchanges in culture, ideology, ideas, art, and other spiritual fields were also increasing. On this great river, the generosity of the northern people and the gentleness of those living in the south had been integrating and influencing each other, thus, the canal culture belt prospered. Over the past 2,500 years, the breadth and inclusiveness of the Grand Canal have connected the South and the North. Its prosperity and vitality gave birth to many rich cities along the route.

The Grand Canal has also deeply influenced people's daily life. The ever-flowing canal water has been nourishing the people living on both banks of the river and irrigating their farmland; water transportation was convenient, the canal wharves, towns, markets, shops, manual workshops gradually rose; the salt, tea, and silk industries along the route were developing; ships were traveling along the river with many merchants onboard—what a bustling and prosperous scene! It is the bright water of the canal that has given rise to the rich regional culture, water culture, ship culture, and merchant culture, as well as rich folk art, exquisite craftsmanship, profound traditional customs, and the culture along the route has been full of vitality for thousands of years.

The Grand Canal records the beautiful and splendid Chinese history and culture and witnesses the long history of Chinese civilization and the diligence and wisdom of the Chinese nation. Nowadays, with the proposal of the Belt and Road Initiative and the Yangtze River Economic Belt Development Plan, the Grand Canal has gained new opportunities. The Chinese government has issued the Outline on the Protection, Inheritance, and Utilization of Grand Canal Culture, which lays out plans for the protection of the Grand Canal, analyzes the existing problems, explores the essence of fine traditional canal culture. Efforts will be made in the cultural heritage protection, ecological development, river drainage management, intangible cultural heritage inheritance, and cultural tourism to form a new model of regional development and let the Grand Canal culture become vivid and popular.

The canal not only has a long and great history, but also a bright future. Chinese people will cherish history and maintain the charm of the river in the new era so that the Grand Canal culture and ecology continue to develop.

生词表

生词

1.	蜿蜒	wānyán	meandering
2.	更迭	gēngdié	to change
3.	流淌	liútǎng	to flow
4.	开凿	kāizáo	to excavate
5.	动脉	dòngmài	artery
6.	延伸	yánshēn	to stretch
7.	扩展	kuòzhǎn	to expand
8.	交融	jiāoróng	to blend
9.	衍生	yǎnshēng	to derive
10.	精湛	jīngzhàn	exquisite
11.	倡议	chàngyì	initiative
12.	内涵	nèihán	connotation
13.	敬畏	jìngwèi	to revere
14.	神韵	shényùn	romantic charm (in literature and art)

成语、俗语、惯用语等

1.	宏伟诗篇	hóngwěi shīpiān	grand poem
2.	大漠孤烟	dàmò gūyān	lonely smoke in the vast desert, a sense of emptiness and remoteness
3.	小桥流水	xiǎoqiáo liúshuǐ	water flowing beneath a little bridge—typical scene of a water town

4.	熙熙攘攘	xīxī-rǎngrǎng	bustling with activity
5.	源远流长	yuányuǎn-liúcháng	long-standing and well-established
6.	生生不息	shēngshēng-bùxī	multiply in an endless succession

语法点

1. 对比手法：把对立的意思或事物放在一起做比较。运用这种手法可以显示事物的矛盾，突出被表现事物的本质特征，加强文章的艺术效果和感染力。

例句：北方大漠孤烟的豪爽与南方小桥流水的柔和在运河之上相互交融，彼此影响。

2. 递进手法：指的是将意思一层又一层地展现出来。层层递进的重点往往位于最后一句话。

例句：运河不能只有沧桑的回忆，更要有光辉的未来。

课文结构分析

请根据这个思维导图，用完整的句子对课文进行复述。

- 大运河
  - 大运河
    - 中国华北平原
    - 南北走向
    - 三段
      - 京杭大运河
      - 隋唐大运河
      - 浙东运河
    - 流经省市
      - 市：北京、天津
      - 省：河北、山东、河南、安徽、江苏、浙江
    - 连通水系
      - 海河、黄河、淮河、
      - 长江、钱塘江
    - 总长度
      - 近 3200 公里
  - 历史
    - 2500 年
    - 开凿始于春秋时期
    - 工程完成于隋代
    - 繁荣于唐宋
  - 意义
    - 打通南北水上交通
    - 推动贸易往来
    - 促进文化、思想、观念、艺术等的交流
    - 丰富两岸各种文化

练习

1. 根据课文内容填写完成下面的表格。（5 分）

<table>
<tr><td>大运河分为三段</td><td>（1）</td><td>隋唐大运河</td><td>（2）</td></tr>
<tr><td>大运河流经两个市</td><td colspan="2">北京市</td><td>（3）</td></tr>
<tr><td>大运河连通了三条河</td><td>（4）</td><td>（5）</td><td>淮河</td></tr>
</table>

2. 根据课文第③～④段回答下面的问题。（5 分）

（1）在第③段中，哪句话说明了大运河的重要性？（1 分）

（2）在第③段中，大运河开通后，沿岸城市有了什么变化？（1 分）

（3）在第④段中，大运河的开通带动了沿岸哪些行业的发展？（3 分）

3. 根据课文内容，从右边选出最合适的结尾来完成左边的短句。（5 分）

（1）大运河是一部书写在华夏大地上的 □

（2）大运河的开通令贸易往来 □

（3）大运河连通了南方与北方， □

（4）大运河的修建衍生出了运河两岸 □

（5）大运河记录了 □

A. 日益增多。

B. 中国历史文化的壮美和辉煌。

C. 宏伟诗篇。

D. 文化之水。

E. 敬畏历史之心。

F. 也串起了繁荣与生机。

G. 丰富的地域文化。

H. 勃勃生机。

拓展练习

话题活动

观看中央电视台纪录片《大运河》，对大运河这个世界历史文化遗产有全面的认识和了解。

话题讨论

假如你是市长，请以"新时代如何传承好大运河文化"为主题发表一个演讲。演讲内容包括保护文化遗产、完善法律制度、发展文化旅游、建造文化平台（比如博物馆）、民间宣传等，也可以提出自己的观点。要求条理清楚，有针对性和可行性，时间控制在五分钟内。

写作练习

假设你是一家旅行社的导游，要组织一个中国游学活动。你准备写一个宣传文案，来介绍这次游学的行程以及目的地的风景名胜、历史背景或有趣的传说故事。请选一条你熟悉的中国旅游路线来写，500 ～ 700 字，题目自拟。

文化点

郑和下西洋

郑和下西洋是15世纪初开始的一系列海上远航活动。远航活动共进行了七次，首次航行始于1405年，末次航行结束于1433年。由于这次远航活动由郑和担任领队，加上船队驶至婆罗洲以西洋面，所以被称为“郑和下西洋”。郑和下西洋是中国古代规模最大、船只和海员最多、时间最久的海上航行，也是世界历史上极具规模的一系列海上探险活动。郑和下西洋加强了中外文明的交流，促进了当时中国对外界的了解，同时也给后世留下了介绍沿岸国家、沿岸地区情况的地理著作以及航海图。郑和下西洋后，“西洋”一词的含义开始用于泛指海外各国或外国之意。

话题二 文化遗产

教学内容和目标	文化点
1. 了解中国古代遗址的特点和出土文物的历史文化价值。 2. 理解中国文化遗产和旅游的名胜古迹之间的关系。	三星堆，云冈石窟，文化遗产，甲骨文

课文 1　三星堆文物

课前热身

请仔细观察下面这张图片，用两分钟左右的时间描述一下你在图片上看到了什么，以及你对图片的理解。

课文 1

扫一扫，看视频

三星堆文物

黄金面具、青铜人像、青铜尊……是谁把这么多宝贝埋进了祭祀坑？2021 年，距被首次发现近 100 年后，神秘的三星堆再度惊艳世界。

三星堆是哪“三堆”？

不光是出土的文物让人浮想联翩，“三星堆”这个名字也极具神秘色彩。三星堆遗址位于四川省广汉市，是古蜀国文化遗址，距今已有 3000 至 5000 年的历史。三座土台呈直线排列，遥望如夜空中的三颗星辰，所以人们叫它三星堆。考古专家推测，三星堆最早应该是一道城墙，因被人类活动破坏，挖了两个缺口，形成了三个孤堆。

三星堆是外星文明？

1986 年出土的青铜纵目面具眼睛突出，两耳尖耸向两边张开。它难道真的与外星人有关？对此说法专家坚决反对！古书《华阳国志》记载：“蜀侯蚕丛，其目纵，始称王。”意思是说：蜀国的国王蚕丛长着一对“纵目”。可“纵目”到底是什么样子？历代学者百思不得其解，直到三星堆青铜纵目面具出土，这个疑问才算是有了解答。专家推测，这是古蜀人对祖先特点的进一步的“神话”——四川西北部以前严重缺碘，人们容易得甲亢病，这个病的特征就是眼睛突出。瞧，这不正是“纵目”嘛！

三星堆里涮火锅?

都知道四川人酷爱火锅，难道火锅在古蜀时期就已盛行？考古学家说：“这个可以有！”三星堆出土的“陶三足炊器”盘面分内外两层，自带鼎足，外层可盛水置物，足下可生火，它还真可以说是火锅器具的起源之一。

围绕三星堆的谜题远不止这些，奇奇怪怪、可可爱爱的文物带给人们无尽的遐想：

几千年前就有“愤怒的小鸟”同款猪?

黄金面具的另一边到底长什么样?

三星堆的黄金权杖与埃及法老的权杖有何关联?

古蜀国怎么会有如此多的象牙?

“青铜大立人”手上举的是自拍杆吗?

……

对三星堆的探索一直在持续。通过对文物的挖掘、检测、分析，相信在不久的将来，更多答案都将一一揭晓。

Sanxingdui Cultural Relics

Gold masks, bronze figures, bronze statues, such treasures buried in the sacrificial pit have mesmerized people for a long time. In 2021, almost one century after its first discovery, the mysterious Sanxingdui threw surprises again.

The Mysterious Three Mounds of Sanxingdui

The unearthed cultural relics are full of possibilities, and the name "Sanxingdui" is mysterious. The Sanxingdui site, located in Guanghan City, Sichuan Province, is an ancient cultural site of the Shu State that dates back to 3,000 to 5,000 years. The three mounds are arranged in a straight line, like three stars in the night sky, thus the name Sanxingdui (Three-Star Piles). Archaeologists speculate that Sanxingdui could have been a city wall. Since human activities destroyed it, two wide gaps formed and three isolated mounds are visible now.

Is Sanxingdui an Alien Civilization?

The bronze mask with vertical eyes unearthed in 1986 has prominent eyes and two pointed ears. This has led to speculation among the public that it could belong to aliens. Experts disagree! According to *Chronicles of Huayang*, "The Marquis of Shu, Cancong, whose eyes are prominent, became king." Cancong, the king of Shu, has "prominent eyes", but what do "prominent eyes" look like? Scholars of all ages couldn't understand it until the bronze mask of Sanxingdui was unearthed. Experts speculate that this is a "myth" associated with the ancient Shu people about the characteristics of their ancestors. Since ancient times, Northwest Sichuan has been severely iodine deficient, and hyperthyroidism was common. Prominent eyes characterized the disease.

Enjoy Hot Pot in Sanxingdui?

It's common knowledge that Sichuan people love hot pot very much. Was it popular in the ancient Shu period? Archaeologists believe so. A pottery tripod cooker unearthed in Sanxingdui is divided into two layers: the inside and the outside. It has its own tripod. The outer layer can hold water and things, and the foot can sit atop a fire. It is one of the origins of hot pot utensils.

The mysteries surrounding Sanxingdui extend further. Strange and lovable cultural relics bring endless reverie to people.

– Thousands of years ago, did the pig from "Angry Birds" exist?

– What does the missing part of the golden mask look like?

– What is the relationship between the golden scepter of Sanxingdui and the scepter of the Egyptian pharaoh?

– How could ancient Shu have so much ivory?

– Is the hand of "Standing Bronze Giant" holding a selfie stick?

The exploration of Sanxingdui has been ongoing. The excavation, detection, and analysis of cultural relics will illuminate some of the site's mysteries.

生词表

生词

1. 惊艳	jīngyàn	striking; amazing
2. 遥望	yáowàng	look into the distance
3. 碘	diǎn	iodine
4. 酷爱	kù'ài	be very fond of
5. 鼎足	dǐngzú	the three legs of a tripod
6. 远不止	yuǎn bùzhǐ	far more than

7. 遐想	xiáxiǎng	indulge in fanciful thoughts
8. 权杖	quánzhàng	scepter
9. 自拍杆	zìpāigān	selfie stick
10. 挖掘	wājué	to dig
11. 检测	jiǎncè	to monitor
12. 分析	fēnxī	to analyze
13. 揭晓	jiēxiǎo	to reveal

成语、俗语、惯用语等

1. 浮想联翩	fúxiǎng-liánpiān	with thoughts flooding one's mind
2. 神秘色彩	shénmì sècǎi	an air of mystery
3. 百思不得其解	bǎi sī bù dé qí jiě	still unable to solve a problem after long pondering

语法点

1. 不光……也……：表示递进关系的关联词。

例句：不光是出土的文物让人浮想联翩，"三星堆"这个名字也极具神秘色彩。

2. 难道：反问词。以难道开头的问句为反问句，是用疑问的句式表达肯定的观点，只是语气更加强烈，更能引起深思。

例句：它难道真的与外星人有关？

课文结构分析

请根据这个思维导图，用完整的句子对课文进行复述。

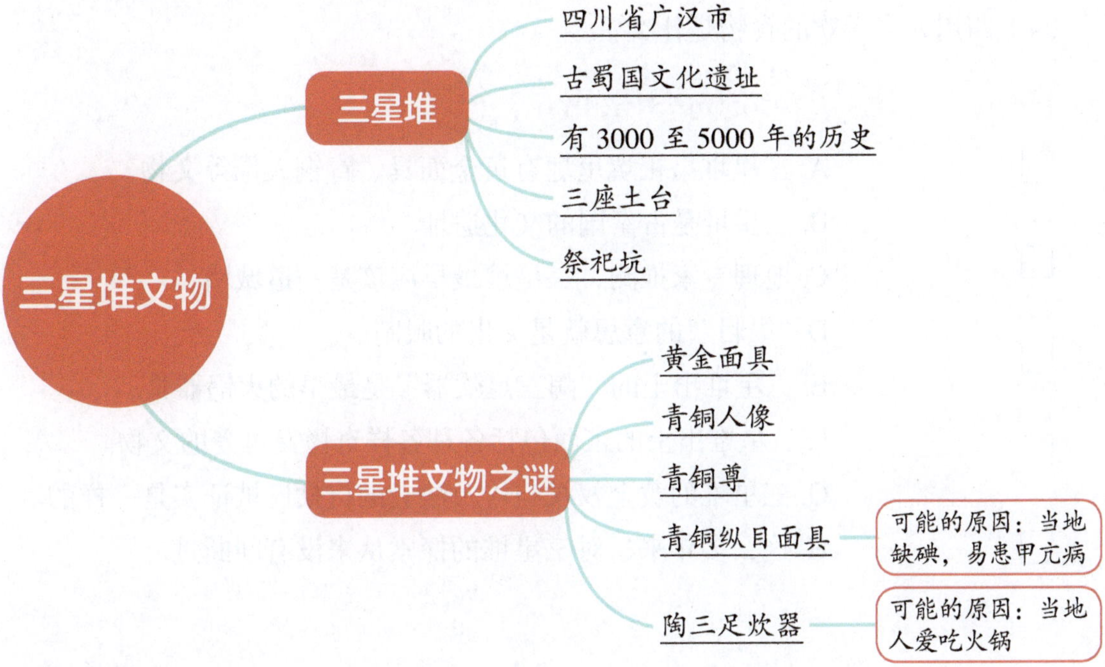

练习

1. 根据课文内容，将左边的词语和右边的近义词搭配起来。（5 分）

（1）浮想联翩 □

（2）遥望 □

（3）百思不得其解 □

（4）遐想 □

（5）揭晓 □

A. 远眺

B. 幻想

C. 大惑不解

D. 解释

E. 思绪万千

F. 想念

G. 公布

2. 根据课文内容回答下面的问题。（5 分）

（1）三星堆至今有多少年的历史？

（2）三星堆出土的青铜纵目面具有什么特征？（2 分）

（3）以前居住在四川西北部的人容易患上什么病？

（4）四川人最喜欢的食物是什么？

3. 根据课文内容，从下面的句子中选出五个正确的表述。（5 分）

□ □ □ □ □

A. 三星堆祭祀坑里埋有黄金面具、青铜人像等文物。

B. 三星堆是古秦国的文化遗址。

C. 地理专家推测，三星堆最早应该是一道城墙。

D. “纵目”的意思就是突出的眼睛。

E. 三星堆出土的“陶三足炊器”是最早的火锅器具。

F. 三星堆出土的东西包括各种各样奇怪又可爱的文物。

G. 三星堆的黄金权杖与埃及法老的权杖已被证实是一样的。

H. 这么多年来，对三星堆的探索从来没有间断过。

课文 2　云冈石窟

课前热身

请仔细观察下面这张图片，用两分钟左右的时间描述一下你在图片上看到了什么，以及你对图片的理解。

课文 2

扫一扫，看视频

云冈石窟

云冈大佛双眸炯炯有神，嘴角略带微笑，雕饰精美，历经 1500 多年历史沧桑依旧傲然于世。

云冈石窟位于中国山西省大同市，石窟依山开凿，东西绵延约 1 公里，存有主要洞窟 45 个，石雕造像 51000 余尊，最大的高达 17 米，最小的仅有几厘米。云冈石窟为中国规模最大的古代石窟群之一，2001 年被列入世界文化遗产名录。

云冈石窟是中国历史上第一个皇家经营的大型石窟。可以说，云冈石窟是石窟艺术“中国化”的开始。公元 398 年，北魏迁都平城，也就是今天的大同。云冈石窟则开凿于公元 460 年—524 年，按石窟形制、造像内容和样式的发展，可分为早期、中期、晚期三个阶段。云冈石窟形象地记录了印度及中亚佛教艺术向中国佛教艺术发展的历史轨迹，反映出佛教造像在中国逐渐世俗化、民族化的过程。

早期石窟（第 16—20 窟）由著名和尚昙曜奉北魏文成帝旨意主持开凿，人称昙曜五窟。五个石窟的中央都雕刻了巨大的如来佛像，象征北魏五朝的五位皇帝，均方额高鼻，大耳垂肩，有早期少数民族的特点，区别于传统印度佛像。

中期石窟是雕凿的鼎盛阶段，也处于北魏最兴盛时期，色彩与雕刻造型追求工整华丽，雕刻艺术特点有异于早期石窟，从洞窟形制到雕刻内容和风格均有明显的汉化特征。中期石窟的佛像比例适中，佛龛、乐伎、舞伎造像生动，服饰带有浓厚的民族风味，同时出现的中国宫殿建筑式样雕刻在后世的石窟建造中得到广泛应用。

北魏迁都洛阳后，皇家在云冈停止了大规模的石窟开凿，但开凿活动在中下阶层蔓延起来，规模虽小，但佛像清瘦俊美，是中国北方石窟艺术“瘦骨清像”的源起，反映出佛教艺术“中国化”的不断深入。

中外多种佛教造像艺术风格在云冈石窟实现了前所未有的融会贯通。气势宏伟、内容丰富的云冈石窟造像堪称公元5世纪中国石刻艺术之冠。

Yungang Grottoes

The exquisitely carved Yungang Buddha sits in meditative silence as a peaceful smile adorns his lips. More than 1,500 years have passed, and he is in mint condition.

Yungang Grottoes are located in Datong City, Shanxi Province, China. The grottoes are carved along the mountain, stretching about one km from east to west. There are 45 main caves and more than 51,000 stone statues. The biggest is 17 meters high, and the smallest is only a few centimeters. Yungang Grottoes, one of the largest ancient grottoes in China, were included on the World Cultural Heritage List in 2001.

Yungang Grottoes were the first large-scale grottoes operated by the royal family in Chinese history. It can be said that Yungang Grottoes were the beginning of the "Sinicization" of grottoes' art. In 398, the Northern Wei Dynasty (386-534) moved its capital to Pingcheng, which is today's Datong. The Yungang Grottoes were carved from 460 to 524 and can be divided into early, middle, and late stages according to the grottoes' shape, content, and style. Yungang Grottoes hold a vivid historical record of the development of Buddhist art from India and Central Asia to Chinese Buddhist art and reflect the process of Buddhist statues gradually becoming secular and nationalized in China.

The early Grottoes construction (Caves 16 to 20) was led by the famous monk Tanyao under the will of Emperor Wencheng of the Northern Wei Dynasty, known as "the Five Caves of Tanyao". The central parts of the five caves have carvings of huge Buddha statues, symbolizing the five emperors of the Northern Wei Dynasty. A square forehead, a high nose, and big earlobes and shoulders are characteristics of early ethnic minorities, which are different from the traditional Indian Buddhist statues.

The mid-period grottoes date back to when carving was at its peak in the prosperous period of the Northern Wei Dynasty. The colors and sculpture shapes are neat and gorgeous. The characteristics of this type of carving is quite different from those of early grottoes. There are traditional Chinese features to the caves' shape and the carvings' content and style. The proportion of Buddha statues is moderate, and the musicians and dancers manifest a patriotic fervor. At the same time,

Chinese palace architecture was also turned into sculptures, widely used in grottoes and temples in later generations.

After the Northern Wei Dynasty moved its capital to Luoyang, the large-scale carving of the grottoes stopped, but the middle and lower classes took up the art form. Although the scale was relatively small, the Buddha statues were thin and beautiful, which was the origin of the "thin bones and clear images" of the grottoes in northern China, reflecting further "Sinicization" of Buddhist art.

Various styles of Buddhist statues at home and abroad have been unprecedentedly adopted and integrated in Yungang Grottoes. The magnificent and colorful statues in Yungang Grottoes can be regarded as the best stone carving art in China in the 5th century.

生词表

生词

1. 石窟	shíkū	rock cave
2. 绵延	miányán	stretch long and unbroken
3. 经营	jīngyíng	to manage
4. 迁都	qiāndū	move the capital to another place
5. 轨迹	guǐjì	trace
6. 世俗化	shìsúhuà	secularization
7. 和尚	héshang	Buddhist monk
8. 旨意	zhǐyì	decree

9.	雕凿	diāozáo	carving
10.	鼎盛	dǐngshèng	at the height of power and splendor
11.	佛龛	fókān	niche for an image/statue of Buddha
12.	乐伎	yuèjì	musical player
13.	舞伎	wǔjì	dance performer
14.	蔓延	mànyán	to spread

成语、俗语、惯用语等

1.	炯炯有神	jiǒngjiǒng-yǒushén	(of eyes) bright and piercing
2.	傲然于世	àorányúshì	stand firm and erect
3.	前所未有	qiánsuǒwèiyǒu	unprecedented
4.	融会贯通	rónghuì-guàntōng	gain a thorough understanding of something

语法点

位于：介词，后接说明地点的专有名词或表述序数的词语。表示占据某个相对低点或位置。

例句：云冈石窟位于中国山西省大同市。

课文结构分析

请根据这个思维导图，用完整的句子对课文进行复述。

- 云冈石窟
  - 地理位置
    - 中国山西省大同市
  - 云冈石窟
    - 世界文化遗产
    - 公元 5 世纪中国石刻艺术之冠
    - 中国规模最大的古代石窟群之一
    - 主要洞窟 45 个
      - 石雕造像 51000 余尊
        - 最大的 17 米高
        - 最小的几厘米
  - 石窟建设
    - 开凿于公元 460 年—524 年
    - 依山开凿
    - 东西绵延约 1 公里
    - 分三期完成
      - 早期：著名和尚昙曜主持开凿
      - 中期：雕凿的鼎盛阶段
      - 晚期：规模小，但佛像清瘦俊美

练习

1. 根据课文内容选择正确答案。（5 分）

（1）根据课文第①段，云冈大佛有什么特征？ □

A. 哈哈大笑

B. 庄严肃穆

C. 神态端庄

D. 眼睛发亮

（2）根据课文第②段，下面哪一个说法是正确的？ □

A. 云冈石窟里最高的石雕为 17 米

B. 云冈石窟大小洞窟共有 45 个

C. 云冈石窟的石雕造像不到 51000 尊

D. 云冈石窟里最小的石雕仅有几米高

（3）根据课文第③段，云冈石窟最早的开凿时间是________。 □

A. 公元 3 世纪

B. 公元 4 世纪

C. 公元 5 世纪

D. 公元 6 世纪

（4）根据课文第④段，早期石窟包括了多少如来佛雕像？ □

A. 2 个

B. 3 个

C. 4 个

D. 5 个

（5）根据课文第⑤段，中期石窟的特征包括________。 □

A. 有汉化特征

B. 方额高鼻

C. 大耳垂肩

D. 清瘦俊美

2. 根据课文内容，从右边选出最合适的结尾来完成左边的短句。（5 分）

（1）虽然历经了 1500 多年历史沧桑， □

（2）云冈石窟是中国历史上第一个 □

（3）云冈石窟反映出佛教造像 □

（4）中期石窟的色彩和造型 □

（5）晚期石窟开凿活动 □

A. 追求工整华丽。

B. 在中国逐渐世俗化和民族化的过程。

C. 云冈石窟依旧傲然于世。

D. 在中下阶层蔓延起来。

E. 中国北方石窟艺术“瘦骨清像”的源起。

F. 皇家经营的大型石窟。

G. 中国宫殿建筑式样雕刻。

3. 用课文中的词语填空。（5分）

（1）__________数公里的沙漠没有一棵树，也没有一根小草。（第②段）

（2）经过几年__________，姐姐的服装店的生意越来越好。（第③段）

（3）学校的游泳__________被李大明打破了。（第③段）

（4）大学四年让弟弟在待人处事方面有了__________的进步。（第⑤段）

（5）这次山火的迅速__________，导致许多人死亡。（第⑥段）

拓展练习

话题活动

观看纪录片《中国记忆》中的《中国的世界文化遗产》和纪录片《中国世界文化遗产》，了解中国的文化遗产。

话题讨论

有人说城市化常常会对文化遗产的保护产生不利影响，如对历史建筑与遗址的空间压迫。上网搜集相关资料，分小组讨论“如何平衡城市化发展与文化遗产保护的关系”，请说明观点和论据。

写作练习

很多古迹都遭到不同程度的损毁，有的是被自然侵蚀，有的是被人为破坏。现在，人们尝试用现代科学技术来保护古迹，请你搜集资料，写一篇500～700字的文章，总结人们是用哪些科技来保护历史文化遗产的，题目自拟。

文化点

甲骨文

甲骨文，距今已有3000余年，是中国的古老文字。中国商朝晚期，王室在龟甲或兽骨上刻字占卜记事。这些刻有文字的龟甲或兽骨也就成为中国及东亚已知最早的文字载体。甲骨文具有对称和稳定的结构，同时具备书法的三个要素，即用笔、结字、章法。从字体的数量和结构方式来看，甲骨文已经发展成了有较严密系统的文字，但是原始图画文字的痕迹及其象形意义还都比较明显。截至2022年11月，中国甲骨文发现总计约15万片，单字数量已逾4000字。甲骨文不仅是研究中国文字来源的最早且有系统的资料，同时也是人们研究甲骨文书法的重要财富。

话题三 发明

教学内容和目标	文化点
1. 了解中国古代四大发明的年代和特点。 2. 理解中国古代四大发明对世界文明的贡献。	中医药，火药，四大发明

课文 1　傣族医药

课前热身

请仔细观察下面这张图片，用两分钟左右的时间描述一下你在图片上看到了什么，以及你对图片的理解。

课文 1

扫一扫，看视频

傣族医药

2021 年 10 月，联合国生物多样性大会在云南昆明召开，大会取得了很多令人瞩目的成果。参会的人们既饱览了云南繁盛的花海，又享受了云南诱人的美食。但你可知道，这眼中所见、口中所尝，里面可能都有“药”？

没错，正是“傣药”。

中国的傣族主要生活在云南省，其传统医药发展长达千年，是中国四大民族医药之一。傣医用药既有内服也有外用，其中还有一些独特的治疗方法，例如直接让患者睡在药上这种神奇疗法。而所有这些都离不开大自然的馈赠——云南丰富的药用植物资源。

云南省西双版纳傣族自治州是中国热带生态系统保存最完整的地区，西双版纳的热带雨林是公认的“世界自然基因库”。傣药的生长与生物多样性环境密不可分，每一个傣族寨子都是一个长满了傣药材的生物多样性群落。连傣家人作为木柴使用的铁刀木都是一味傣药，具有清热、止血、化瘀的功效，还可以治疗胃痛。雨林中野生的兰花种类繁多，几乎所有品种的兰花均可入药。西双版纳的热带雨林中，现在已知的傣药品种达 2000 余种。傣族家庭每年食物中的药用植物都不少于百种，久而久之，傣家人长寿者就很多。

经过上千年的实践，傣家人总结出傣药的疗效与其生长环境密切相关，例如：凡生长在悬崖陡壁和带肿节的植物，大都可治疗骨折、跌打损伤等病症；凡生长在湖泊、水边的植物，大都可用于治疗风湿麻木、水肿等病症；凡开红花、带红色的植物，多可用来补血和止血；凡开白花、流白浆的植物，多可用来镇静安神、解毒。

可见，生物多样性是傣族医药的立身之本。在社会经济发展的过程中，云南村寨的生物多样性曾遭到一定程度的破坏。如今，云南积极“退胶还林”。以曼远村为例，家家户户在退出的橡胶林地和香蕉地上种植可用于傣药的高山植物，缓解了土地退化，有助于傣族医药的发展，同时达到了让村民增收致富的“多赢”效果。

10月22日是“世界传统医药日”，这个特殊的日子旨在促进和弘扬传统医药的价值和作用，并提高人们对传统医药的认识和理解。“世界传统医药日”的设立有助于保护和传承传统医药文化，同时也提醒人们传统医药在保障身体健康、战胜疾病方面的重要性和影响力。

Dai Medicine

In October 2021, the UN Biodiversity Conference was held in Kunming, Yunnan Province, and saw great achievements. A sea of flowers and attractive Yunnan cuisine on the table stole the show. But do you know what they saw or tasted had a therapeutic effect?

Yes, it's "Dai medicine".

The Dai people in China live mainly in Yunnan Province where traditional medicine has developed for thousands of years. It is one of the four major ethnic medicines in China. Dai medicine has both internal and external uses, including some unique treatment methods. For example, they let the patients sleep directly on the medicine. Yunnan's rich medicinal plant resources are a gift from nature.

The Dai Autonomous Prefecture of Xishuangbanna, Yunnan Province is the region with the most intact tropical ecosystem in China. The tropical rain forest in Xishuangbanna is recognized as the "world natural gene bank". The growth of Dai medicinal herbs is closely related to the biodiversity environment. Every Dai stockade is a biodiversity community full of Dai medicinal herbs. Even the Cassia siamea Lam wood commonly used by the Dai family as firewood is a Dai medicine, which has the effects of clearing heat, hemostasis and removing blood stasis and can treat stomach pain. There are many kinds of wild orchids in the rainforest. Almost all kinds of orchids can be used as medicine. There are more than 2,000 known Dai medicine varieties in the tropical rainforests of Xishuangbanna. Dai families have more than 100 kinds of medicinal plants in their food every year. It is no wonder why Dai people live longer.

After thousands of years of practice, Dai people have concluded that the curative effect of Dai medicine is closely related to its growth environment. For example, plants that grow on cliffs and steep walls and with swollen joints can be mostly used to treat fractures and other bone injuries. Most of the plants grown near lakes and water can be used to treat rheumatism, numbness and edema; most of the plants with red flowers can be used to replenish *qi* and blood and stop bleeding; the plants with white flowers and white pulp can be used to calm the nerves and detoxify.

It can be seen that biodiversity is the foundation of Dai medicine. In the process of economic and social development, the biodiversity of Yunnan villages has also been damaged to some extent. Now, Yunnan is actively "converting rubber plantations back to the natural forest". Taking Manyuan Village, which has very primitive characteristics, every household has planted alpine medicinal plants on the withdrawn rubber and banana plantations. This has alleviated land degradation and contributed to the development of Dai medicine. At the same time, it has achieved the "win-win" goal of increasing villagers' income.

October 22 is the World Traditional Medicine Day, a special day aimed at promoting the value and role of traditional medicine, as well as raising people's awareness and understanding of it. The setting of the "World Traditional Medicine Day" helps protect and carry forward traditional medicine culture, which also reminds people of the importance and influence of traditional medicine in maintaining health and overcoming illness.

生词表

生词

1. 傣药	dǎiyào	Dai medicine
2. 药用植物资源	yàoyòng zhíwù zīyuán	medicinal plant resources
3. 热带生态	rèdài shēngtài	tropical ecology
4. 热带雨林	rèdài yǔlín	tropical rainforest
5. 基因库	jīyīnkù	gene pool
6. 群落	qúnluò	community
7. 清热	qīngrè	clear heat
8. 化瘀	huàyū	reduce stasis
9. 疗效	liáoxiào	curative effect
10. 骨折	gǔzhé	bone fracture
11. 跌打损伤	diēdǎ sǔnshāng	injuries from falls and knocks
12. 风湿麻木	fēngshī mámù	rheumatism and numbness
13. 镇静安神	zhènjìng ānshén	calm down and soothe the nerves
14. 解毒	jiědú	to detoxify
15. 缓解	huǎnjiě	to alleviate
16. 退化	tuìhuà	to degenerate
17. 致富	zhìfù	become better off
18. 弘扬	hóngyáng	develop and expand

成语、俗语、惯用语等

1. 令人瞩目	lìng rén zhǔmù	impressive
2. 密不可分	mìbùkěfēn	inseparable
3. 久而久之	jiǔ’érjiǔzhī	as time goes by
4. 密切相关	mìqiè xiāngguān	closely related
5. 悬崖陡壁	xuányá dǒubì	steep cliff
6. 立身之本	lìshēnzhīběn	the foundation of

语法点

连……都是……：关联词，强调的是不可能完成的事情或不可能的东西居然是真实存在的。

例句： 连傣家人作为木柴使用的铁刀木都是一味傣药。

课文结构分析

请根据这个思维导图，用完整的句子对课文进行复述。

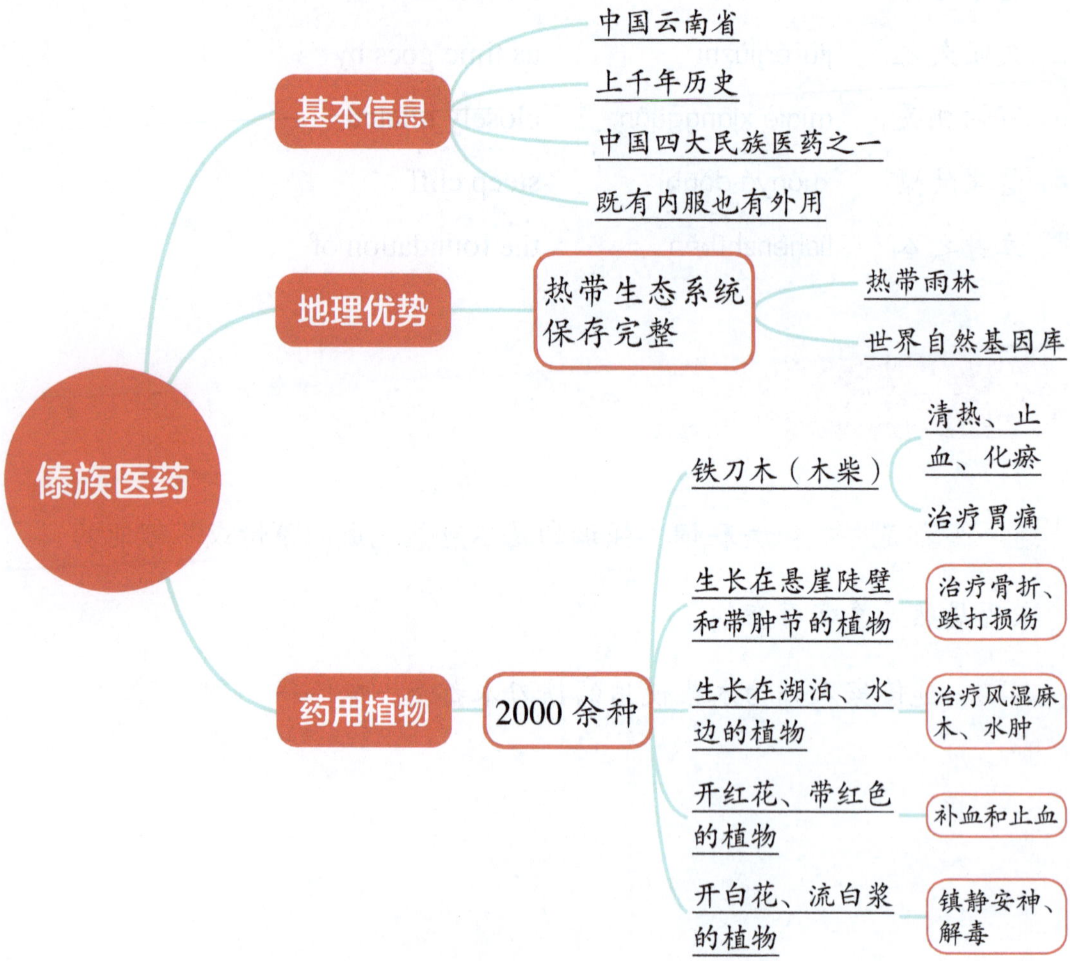

练习

1. 根据课文内容选出五个正确的表述。（5分）

□ □ □ □ □

A. 一种傣族医药治疗方法是：躺在药上就可以治病。

B. 西双版纳位于中国气候比较热的雨林地区。

C. 只有一个傣族寨子长满了傣药材。

D. 雨林中野生的兰花全部都可以用作傣药。

E. 傣族家庭每年食物中的药用植物达2000余种。

F. 开红花、带红色的植物基本上都可用来补血和止血。

G. 经济发展曾经令云南村寨的生物多样性遭到了一定程度的破坏。

H.“世界传统医药日”定于每年的10月22日。

2. 根据课文内容回答下面的问题。（5分）

（1）傣药的使用方式有哪几种？（2分）

（2）为什么西双版纳的热带雨林被称为“世界自然基因库”？（1分）

（3）傣族医药的立身之本是什么？（1分）

（4）发展傣族医药对当地村民有什么好处？（1分）

3. 请把左边的词语和右边的解释对应起来。（5分）

（1）令人瞩目	□	A. 经过很长时间
		B. 受到损害
（2）密不可分	□	C. 吸引别人的关注
（3）久而久之	□	D. 基本上
		E. 严守秘密
（4）大都	□	F. 无法分开
（5）破坏	□	G. 互相关切

课文 2　中国烟花

课前热身

请仔细观察下面这张图片，用两分钟左右的时间描述一下你在图片上看到了什么，以及你对图片的理解。

课文 2

扫一扫，看视频

中国烟花

在中国，以火药制作的烟花爆竹有着悠久的历史，在世界上享有盛誉。

直到今天，每逢重大节庆活动，燃放焰火依然是重头戏。2019 年 10 月 1 日晚，庆祝新中国成立 70 周年联欢活动在天安门广场举行。多种形式的焰火表演与音乐交织，以夜空为幕，描绘出了一幅幅震撼人心的盛世图景。首次特别制作的高难度特效焰火“人民万岁”三次连续绽放，数字特效烟花打出“70”的数字，标志新中国成立 70 周年。

7 棵约 25 米高、160 多米宽、可变幻、多面体的烟花树象征成立 70 年的新中国枝繁叶茂。这些烟花树是本次焰火表演中新技术突破的其中一项，也是在世界上的首次亮相。这些特效烟花均是高科技环保焰火产品，主要产自湖南、江西、河北等地，所用药剂不含重金属物质，硫含量也很低。

看似传统的焰火如今俨然成为了当代艺术。国庆焰火总设计师蔡国强就是一位焰火艺术家。他大胆地将焰火和绘画结合，表达着对自我和世界的思考：2008 年北京奥运会的“脚印踏来”、2011 年多哈的“黑色礼花”、2014 年上海外滩的“白日焰火”，都出自蔡国强之手。最著名的作品则是他在老家泉州完成的“天梯”。这个作品充满中国式的浪漫主义。

中国是世界上最早发明火药的国家。1000多年前，中国古人从炼丹起火中认识并发明了火药。作为中国古代四大发明之一，火药经过爱好和平的中国人不断传承与创新，发展为今天的焰火艺术。它将科技、环保和艺术相结合，用独特的方式为喜庆活动增光添彩。

Chinese Fireworks

In China, fireworks made of gunpowder have a long history.

Today, any major celebration is incomplete without fireworks leading it to a grand finale. An awe-inspiring spectacle was seen at Tian'anmen Square on October 1, 2019 during the celebration of the 70th anniversary of the founding of the People's Republic of China. All kinds of fireworks on display lit up the night sky as musical notes were heard in the background. For the first time, special effects fireworks were used that went off in the sky to form the words "Long Live the People" three times in succession amid tremendous applause. Digital effect fireworks also went on to form the double digits "70" to mark New China stepping into its 70th year.

Seven polyhedral fireworks trees, about 25 meters high and 160 meters wide, were put up to show the prosperity in China. This was the first time that the breakthrough technology of fireworks trees was showcased to the world. These special effect fireworks were produced mainly in Hunan, Jiangxi, and Hebei provinces, with no heavy metals and low sulfur, thus environmentally friendly.

Traditional fireworks are now a type of modern and contemporary art. Cai Guoqiang, the chief designer of National Day firework performance, is a firework artist. He boldly combines fireworks with art to express his thoughts. His art Footprints of History was on display at the 2008 Beijing Olympic Games, the Black Fireworks in Doha in 2011, and the daytime fireworks at the Bund of Shanghai in 2014. His most famous work is Sky Ladder displayed in his hometown of Quanzhou. His art is full of Chinese Romanticism.

Gunpowder was invented in China. More than 1,000 years ago, Chinese alchemists discovered flying fire and invented gunpowder. As one of the four greatest inventions of ancient China, it has been preserved and innovated by the peace-loving Chinese people and has developed into the eclectic art of fireworks. A blend of science, technology, environmental awareness, and artistry, gunpowder adds unique flavor to joyous events in its own way.

生词表

生词

1. 火药	huǒyào	gunpowder
2. 烟花爆竹	yānhuā bàozhú	fireworks and firecrackers

3. 焰火	yànhuǒ	fireworks
4. 重头戏	zhòngtóuxì	major part (of sth); major activity
5. 交织	jiāozhī	to interweave
6. 震撼	zhènhàn	to shake; to shock
7. 特效	tèxiào	specially good effect
8. 枝繁叶茂	zhīfán-yèmào	be thriving
9. 重金属	zhòngjīnshǔ	heavy metal
10. 俨然	yǎnrán	just like
11. 浪漫主义	làngmàn zhǔyì	romanticism
12. 炼丹	liàndān	alchemy; training of active substance

成语、俗语、惯用语等

1. 享有盛誉	xiǎngyǒu shèngyù	renowned
2. 盛世图景	shèngshì tújǐng	prosperous picture

课文结构分析

请根据这个思维导图，用完整的句子对课文进行复述。

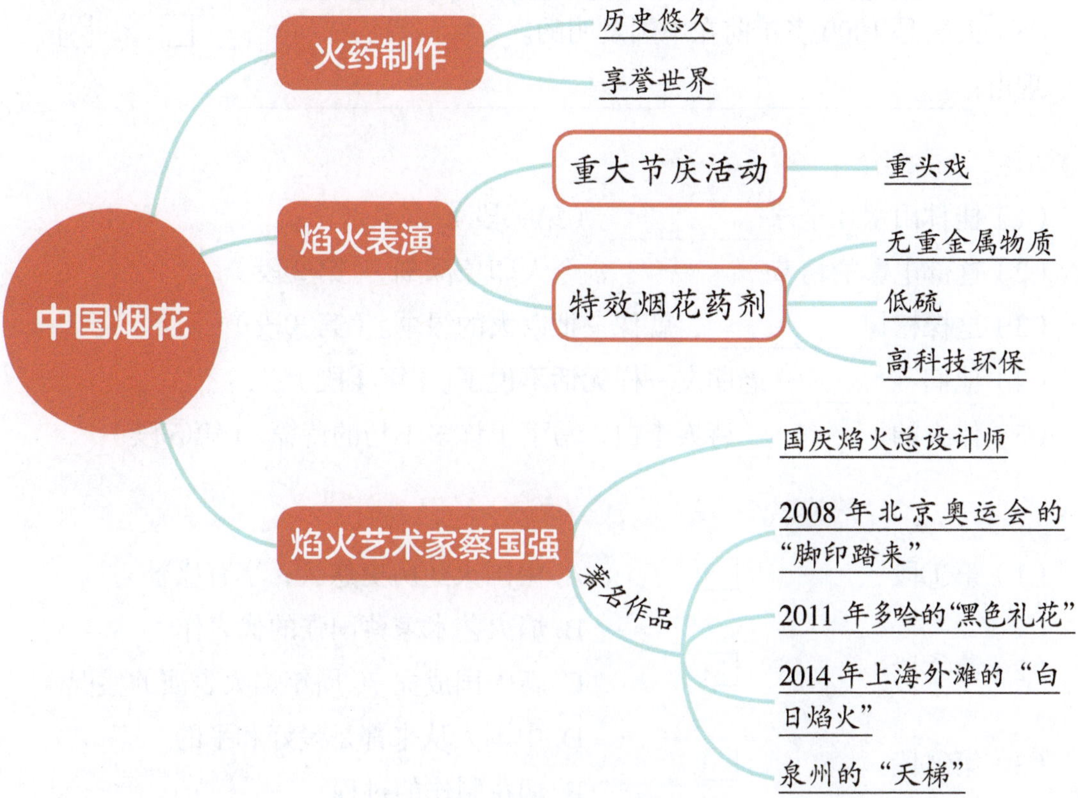

练习

1. 根据课文内容判断下列说法的对错，并写出理由。（5 分）

	对	错
（1）中国很久以前就开始用火药制作烟花爆竹。	□	□
理由：＿＿＿＿＿＿＿＿＿＿＿＿＿＿＿＿＿＿		
（2）焰火表演的时候没有音乐伴奏。	□	□
理由：＿＿＿＿＿＿＿＿＿＿＿＿＿＿＿＿＿＿		

（3）烟花表演时，人们可以在夜空中看到文字。 □ □

理由：______________________________

（4）中国使用的焰火会造成严重的空气污染。 □ □

理由：______________________________

（5）火药是 1000 多年前在中国发明的。 □ □

理由：______________________________

2. 用课文中的词语填空。（5 分）

（1）桂林山水在全球________。（第①段）

（2）这部电影的情节________，令人印象深刻。（第②段）

（3）这棵榕树________，就像一把巨大的绿伞。（第③段）

（4）他们________老朋友一样无话不说了。（第④段）

（5）伟大的________诗人李白，写下了许多不朽的诗篇。（第⑤段）

3. 请将左边的段落号码与右边的段意对应起来。（5 分）

（1）第①段 □

（2）第②段 □

（3）第③段 □

（4）第④段 □

（5）第⑤段 □

A. 中国火药历史悠久，享有盛誉

B. 焰火艺术家蔡国强的代表作

C. 新中国成立 70 周年焰火表演的盛况

D. 中国人从来都是爱好和平的

E. 烟花制作的过程

F. 高科技环保焰火产品

G. 特效烟花产地介绍

H. 中国将自己发明的火药发展为焰火艺术

4. 上网找资料，写出中国古代四大发明和中国“新四大发明”。

中国古代四大发明	中国“新四大发明”

拓展练习

话题活动

观看“中华文明之美”系列视频第 251 集—254 集，了解并讲述中国古代的四大发明。

话题讨论

以“中国古代四大发明对世界的影响”为主题，分小组上网查找资料，做成 PPT，并向全班同学进行演示。

写作练习

当今社会，科学技术日新月异，现在的科技产品放在 30 年前简直不可想象。目前也有很多科学技术处在萌芽阶段，请你大胆假设一下 30 年后的科技会发展到什么程度，并以 30 年后的身份给现在的你写一封信，用 500 ～ 700 字介绍一下那时人类的科技生活。

文化点

中医药

中医药是中国人民在几千年生产生活实践和与疾病做斗争的过程中逐步形成并不断发展的医药科学。中医药不仅是中华文明的象征，也对世界文明进步产生了积极影响。中医诊断主要由医生通过望、闻、问、切等方法收集患者资料，治疗方法除了中药，还有针灸、推拿、拔罐、刮痧等非药物疗法。中药为中国传统中医特有药物。它的主要来源是天然药及其加工品，包括植物药和动物药等。植物药在中药中占了绝大部分，这些天然植物药材的分布和当地的地理和气候等自然条件有很大的关系。中医药在历史发展进程中逐渐形成了独特的生命观、健康观、疾病观、防治观，实现了自然科学与人文科学的融合和统一，蕴含了中华民族深邃的哲学思想。

话题四 艺术

教学内容和目标	文化点
1. 了解并欣赏中国京剧艺术的特点和独特美感。 2. 了解并欣赏中国剪纸艺术的特点和独特美感。	书法字体，笔墨纸砚，京剧，脸谱，剪纸，中国画

课文 1　京剧脸谱

课前热身

请仔细观察下面这张图片，用两分钟左右的时间描述一下你在图片上看到了什么，以及你对图片的理解。

课文 1

扫一扫，看视频

京剧脸谱

中国京剧之美不仅体现在其腔调之上，它独特的美学风格、造型艺术也是其中重要的组成部分。华丽的服饰、五色的脸谱是京剧留给人们的第一印象。京剧中“净”行（花脸）变化多端的脸谱不仅呈现出独特的审美取向，更通过色彩和线条的有机结合表达强烈的情感偏好，并以此展现出人物的年龄、性情、品格甚至命运走向。

京剧脸谱作为京剧艺术的“表情符号”，具有很强的装饰性和形式美感，是中国传统文化内涵视觉化的体现。它吸收了中国传统美学中的“重神似而不重形似”，注重“变形”“传神”“寓意”。脸谱的勾画笔法也与中国画笔法相通，一个点有深重、清浅之分，一条线有粗细、疏密之分。再加之不同含义的色彩绘制在不同图案轮廓里，脸谱就把人物性格化了，或端庄沉稳，或邪恶奸诈，以夸张、美化、变形、象征等艺术夸张手法来寓褒贬、分善恶，让人一目了然。

比如悲剧人物西楚霸王项羽，寿字眉，面带哭丧，虽威严肃穆，却也预示着兵败垓下、自刎乌江的命运；再如关羽，“面如重枣”，红脸代表英勇忠贞；又如夏侯渊，《定军山》中的人物，曹操手下大将，通天纹勾长“寿”字，显得鼻梁突起，人物形象更加雄壮。

历经百年发展与传播，京剧脸谱成为中国传统文化中经典且具有代表性的文化艺术之一。京剧脸谱因其独特的造型和丰富的文化内涵而成为中国传统文化的标识之一。文化交融也让京剧脸谱大放异彩，渗透至现代美学的方方面面，为现代设计注入新鲜的血液。

Peking Opera Facial Makeup

Peking Opera's charm lies in its unique vocal performance, distinct aesthetic styles, and modeling features. Gorgeous costumes and colorful facial makeup, or *lianpu*, are the first impressions people generally have on Peking Opera. Among the roles on the Peking Opera stage, *jing*, popularly known as *hualian*, is especially renowned for its diverse facial makeup. Apart from their unique aesthetic styles, facial makeup can also express strong emotional preferences through the combination of colors and paint lines. Thus, the audience can glimpse the age, personality, morality, and even fate of certain roles on the stage through their symbolic facial makeup.

As the "emoticon" of Peking Opera, facial makeup can play outstanding decorative and aesthetic roles through visualizing the quintessence of traditional Chinese culture. By adhering to the traditional Chinese aesthetic principle of "focusing on similarities in style rather than in shape", face painting attaches great importance to "the transformation of shapes", "lifelikeness", and "allusion". Face painting has its own patterns. Lines can be thick or thin, dots can be heavy black or light-colored, and the pattern of lines can be intense or sparse. Colors with different connotations combined with various painting shapes can demonstrate the personalities of different roles: some are elegant and sedate, while others are cunning and treacherous. Through artistic exaggeration, beautification, transformation, and symbolism, face-painting can praise benevolence, satirize treacherousness, and help the audience get a glimpse of the personalities of certain roles.

The facial makeup of Xiang Yu, a tragic hero in ancient China, is featured with heavy eyebrows and mournful expression, which foretells his ultimate fate of military failure and suicide. The facial makeup of Guan Yu looks like a "red date", and the red color here symbolizes bravery and loyalty. Xiahou Yuan, a figure in *The Battle of Mount Dingjun*, was a trustworthy general of Cao Cao. His facial makeup is featured with intense and extended lines and a high nose, depicting a towering and imposing figure.

After its development and popularization over centuries, the Peking Opera facial makeup is now one of the most classical and representative arts in traditional Chinese culture. With its unique patterns and rich cultural connotations, the Peking Opera facial makeup has become one of the marks of traditional Chinese culture. It has comprehensively influenced modern aesthetics through cultural exchanges, which brought fresh insights and inspiration for modern design.

生词表

生词

1.	脸谱	liǎnpǔ	type of facial makeup in traditional Chinese operas
2.	腔调	qiāngdiào	tune
3.	独特	dútè	unique
4.	风格	fēnggé	style
5.	印象	yìnxiàng	impression
6.	审美	shěnměi	appreciation of beauty
7.	偏好	piānhào	have a special fondness for something
8.	表情符号	biǎoqíng fúhào	emoticon
9.	疏密	shūmì	density
10.	轮廓	lúnkuò	outline
11.	端庄沉稳	duānzhuāng chénwěn	dignified and calm
12.	邪恶奸诈	xié'è jiānzhà	evil and treacherous
13.	夸张	kuāzhāng	to exaggerate
14.	褒贬	bāobiǎn	praise and denigration
15.	英勇忠贞	yīngyǒng zhōngzhēn	brave and loyal
16.	通天纹	tōngtiānwén	a type of marking on the forehead seen as a sign of strength and dignity
17.	标识	biāoshí	symbol
18.	渗透	shèntòu	to infiltrate

成语、俗语、惯用语等

1. 变化多端	biànhuà duōduān	constantly changing
2. 重神似而不重形似	zhòng shén sì ér bú zhòng xíng sì	focusing on similarities in style rather than in shape
3. 寓褒贬、分善恶	yù bāobiǎn, fēn shàn'è	signify praise or criticism, and distinguish good from evil
4. 一目了然	yímù-liǎorán	be clear at a glance
5. 兵败垓下	bīngbài-gāixià	defeat at Gaixia—a major failure
6. 大放异彩	dàfàng-yìcǎi	blossom in splendor

课文结构分析

请根据这个思维导图，用完整的句子对课文进行复述。

- 京剧脸谱
  - 京剧之美
    - 腔调
    - 美学风格
    - 造型艺术
  - 脸谱
    - 表情符号
    - 装饰性
    - 形式美感
    - 内涵视觉化
    - 把人物性格化
      - 端庄沉稳
      - 邪恶奸诈
  - 代表人物
    - 项羽
    - 关羽
    - 夏侯渊
  - 意义
    - 经典且具有代表性的中国传统文化艺术之一
    - 中国传统文化的标识之一

练习

1. 根据课文内容选出五个正确的表述。（5 分）

□ □ □ □ □

A. 京剧之美只体现在其腔调之上。
B. 京剧表演的服装非常华丽。
C. 在京剧表演中，脸谱的图案与人物的性格有关。
D. 脸谱的勾画笔法与中国画笔法相通。
E. 西楚霸王项羽，寿字眉，是个命好的人物。
F. 在京剧中，红脸代表邪恶奸诈。
G. 京剧脸谱是经典且具有代表性的中国传统文化艺术之一。
H. 京剧脸谱是中国传统文化的标识之一。

2. 根据课文第②～③段回答下面的问题。（5 分）

（1）京剧脸谱具有哪两个特点？（2 分）

（2）夏侯渊的脸谱形象是怎样的？（1 分）

（3）夏侯渊的脸谱让观众对他有什么观感？（2 分）

3. 请把左边的词语和右边的解释对应起来。（5 分）

（1）（第①段）呈现 □

（2）（第①段）偏好 □

（3）（第①段）走向 □

（4）（第②段）褒贬 □

（5）（第③段）预示 □

A. 特别喜欢
B. 好处
C. 好与不好
D. 展现
E. 走路的方向
F. 向某个方向发展
G. 表示
H. 事发前就显示

4. 上网找出与脸谱各个颜色相对应的人物性格。

颜色	人物性格
红色	
白色	
黑色	
黄色	
蓝色	
绿色	
金色	
银色	

课文 2　剪纸——刀尖上的艺术

课前热身

请仔细观察下面这张图片，用两分钟左右的时间描述一下你在图片上看到了什么，以及你对图片的理解。

课文 2

扫一扫，看视频

剪纸——刀尖上的艺术

阳光透过明亮的玻璃窗照在贴在窗户正中间的红色剪纸窗花上，红红火火，显得格外喜庆。每逢春节，中国人都喜欢贴上窗花，寄托辞旧迎新、接福纳祥的美好愿望。窗花是中国剪纸艺术中最为普及的一种，其他品种都是在窗花的基础上发展起来的。剪纸艺术是中国民间流行的一种用剪刀或刻刀在纸上剪刻花纹，用于装点生活或配合其他民俗活动的艺术形式，历史悠久，流传广泛。

剪纸作为一种传统的民俗艺术形式，在中华大地上已经流传了千年之久。距今2000多年的汉代，“纸”的发明促使了剪纸的出现、发展与普及。到了唐宋时期，剪纸的种类越来越丰富，极富装饰意味的“窗花”“礼花”“灯花”在宋时出现。明清两代是剪纸发展的鼎盛期，剪纸的装饰功能较为突出，已经融入人们的日常生活。

在长期的艺术和生活实践中，中国人凭借自己的聪明才智将剪纸这门艺术形式发展得日趋完善，形成了以剪刻、镂空为主的多种技法，并把剪纸的线条归纳为五个字：圆、尖、方、缺、线，要求达到“圆如秋月、尖如麦芒、方如青砖、缺如锯齿、线如胡须”。可以说线条是剪纸造型的基础。中国民间剪纸从色彩来划分，可以分为单色剪纸和彩色剪纸，单色剪纸一般为红色，因为中国人认为红色代表好运和吉祥。每逢过节或新婚喜庆，人们便将美丽鲜艳的剪纸贴在家中的窗户、墙壁、门和灯笼上，节日的气氛也因此显得更加热烈。

剪纸的题材十分广泛，花、鸟、走兽、人、汉字等都可以在剪纸中看到。这些题材背后蕴藏着深厚的文化底蕴，多以“寓意”的形式呈现，表达人们纳吉祈福的美好愿望。比如，牡丹花象征富贵，荷花象征平安，菊花象征长寿，等等。婚礼上的“囍”字不但可以张贴在门窗上，还可以贴在家具、被褥等各种器物上，并配以各种吉祥的图案，如“龙凤呈祥”“双龙戏珠”，以此来表达对新人幸福美满、早生贵子的祝福。

Paper-cutting—Scissors Art

On a typical Spring Festival day, sunlight filters through windows and the red paper-cuts hanging from them, creating a uniquely joyous atmosphere. The Chinese people love to glue paper-cuts to their windows during the Spring Festival to express their wishes to welcome the new year and receive good fortune. As the most popular form of Chinese paper-cutting, early window paper-cuts also laid the groundwork for the development of other forms of paper-cuts. Paper-cutting is a time-honored popular folk art in China. People use scissors or knives to cut paper into various shapes to serve as decorations or for other folk activities.

Paper-cutting has existed in China for about one thousand years as a traditional popular folk art. The invention of paper in the Han Dynasty (206 BC-AD 220) was instrumental to the birth, development, and spread of the art of paper-cutting. The types of paper-cuts became more diverse during the Tang (618-907) and Song (960-1279) dynasties. More paper-cuts were used for decorative purposes, such as "window paper-cuts", "gift paper-cuts", and "lamp paper-cuts", which emerged in the Song Dynasty. Paper-cutting peaked during the Ming (1368-1644) and Qing (1616-1911) dynasties. During this time, the art was deeply permeated into people's daily lives with its remarkable decorative functions.

Throughout a long history of artistic practice and accumulated life experiences, the Chinese people have developed the art of paper-cutting with their talent. They developed many paper-cutting methods of which cutting and engraving are the most important. They also summarized the tactics of paper-cutting into five words: round, sharp, square, serrated, and straight. According to established standards, paper-cuts should be "as round as the autumn moon, as sharp as the wheat's awn, as square as a blue brick, as serrated as a saw's teeth, and as straight as whiskers". It is widely agreed that lines serve as the foundation for any paper-cut's shape. In terms of the colors of paper used, Chinese paper-cutting can be categorized as single-color paper-cutting and multiple-color paper-cutting. Regarding single-color paper-cutting, the Chinese people prefer to use red paper, as it embodies good luck and auspiciousness. Whenever there are festivals or wedding ceremonies, Chinese people will affix delicate, gorgeous paper-cuts to the windows, walls, doors, and lanterns, creating a jubilant festive atmosphere.

Themes used for paper-cuts are diverse, ranging from flowers, birds, beasts, figures to Chinese characters. These themes have deep cultural connotations and most implicitly express people's aspirations for good luck and happiness. For instance, a peony flower means affluence and prosperity, a lotus symbolizes peace and safety, and a chrysanthemum flower implies longevity. Paper-cuts of the character *xi* (literally meaning "double happiness") are generally used for weddings. They are not only affixed to doors and windows but also to wedding furniture and quilts. They are often cut with various auspicious patterns, such as "Dragon & Phoenix Couple" and "Two Dragons Playing a Bead"— these express people's wishes for a happy, harmonious life and a big family.

生词表

生词

1. 剪纸	jiǎnzhǐ	paper-cut
2. 喜庆	xǐqìng	joyous
3. 装点	zhuāngdiǎn	to decorate
4. 镂空	lòukōng	hollow out
5. 蕴藏	yùncáng	hold in store

成语、俗语、惯用语等

1. 辞旧迎新	cíjiù-yíngxīn	ring out the old year and usher in the new
2. 接福纳祥	jiēfú-nàxiáng	receive good fortune
3. 龙凤呈祥	lóngfèngchéngxiáng	the union of a dragon and a phoenix foretells good fortune
4. 早生贵子	zǎoshēng-guìzǐ	(wish you) have a baby soon

语法点

修辞方法：排比句。排比句是指使用排比修辞方法，把三个或以上意义相关或相近、结构相同或相似、语气相同的词组或句子排列起来组成的句子，能达到一种加强语势的效果。

例如：

（1）圆如秋月，尖如麦芒，方如青砖，缺如锯齿，线如胡须。

（2）牡丹花象征富贵，荷花象征平安，菊花象征长寿。

课文结构分析

请根据这个思维导图，用完整的句子对课文进行复述。

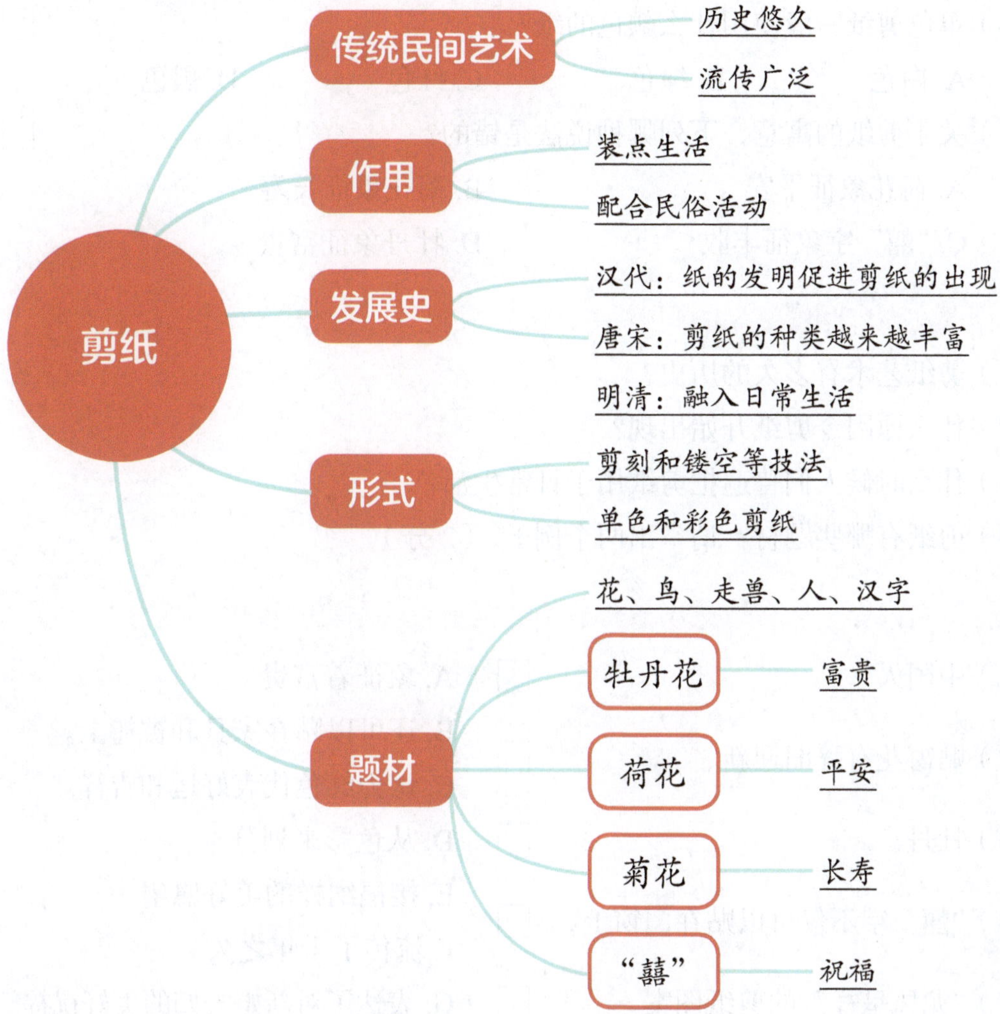

练习

1. 根据课文内容选择正确答案。（5 分）

（1）剪纸艺术常用的工具是________。 ☐

A. 毛笔　　B. 针线　　C. 刻刀　　D. 调色盘

（2）剪纸在哪个朝代发展到顶峰？ □

A. 唐代　B. 宋代　C. 汉代　D. 明代

（3）唐宋时期的剪纸种类不包括________。 □

A. 窗花　B. 礼花　C. 灯花　D. 头花

（4）单色剪纸一般使用什么颜色的纸？ □

A. 白色　B. 绿色　C. 红色　D. 黑色

（5）关于剪纸的寓意，下列哪种说法是错的？ □

A. 荷花象征平安　B. 菊花象征长寿

C.“囍”字象征丰收　D. 牡丹象征富贵

2. 根据课文内容回答下面的问题。（5 分）

（1）剪纸艺术有多久的历史？

（2）什么原因令剪纸开始出现？

（3）什么时候人们普遍把剪纸用于日常生活？

（4）剪纸有哪些题材？请举出两个例子。（2 分）

3. 根据课文内容，从右边选出最合适的结尾来完成左边的短句。（5 分）

（1）中国人 □

（2）贴窗花有辞旧迎新、 □

（3）牡丹 □

（4）“囍”字不仅可以贴在门窗上， □

（5）“龙凤呈祥”的剪纸图案 □

A. 象征着富贵。

B. 还可以贴在家具和被褥上。

C. 认为红色代表好运和吉祥。

D. 从色彩来划分

E. 接福纳祥的美好愿望。

F. 流传了千年之久

G. 表达了对新婚夫妇的美好祝福。

拓展练习

话题活动

活动 A：剪纸制作

上网查找关于剪纸的教学视频，选出自己喜欢的一个图案并学着剪出来。

活动 B：我喜爱的中国剪纸

向全班同学展示自己的剪纸作品，并解释自己选择这个图案的原因，分享制作剪纸的过程和对制作剪纸的感受，比如有趣的方面、困难的方面、有何成就感等，谈谈对剪纸这个中国传统艺术发展前景的看法。

话题讨论

现在，喜欢京剧的年轻人越来越少。你觉得应该怎么做才能使这项中国传统艺术传承下去？请就这个话题采访你的同学，并将采访内容进行整理总结，跟全班同学分享。

写作练习

有人认为既然现在可以通过互联网看到所有的艺术表演和美术作品，那么剧院和博物馆就没有存在的必要了。你是否认同这个观点？请用 500 ～ 700 字写出你的观点，至少写出两个理由。

文化点

中国画

中国画，简称“国画”。国画是中国的传统绘画形式，是用毛笔蘸水、墨、彩色颜料，在绢或宣纸上作画。国画可分为人物画、山水画、花鸟画三种，而技法形式上则有工笔、写意、勾勒、设色、水墨等。从美术史的角度讲，民国前的国画都统称为古画。在古代，国画一般被称为“丹青”。中国画在内容和艺术创作上体现了古人对自然、社会及与之相关联的政治、哲学、宗教、道德、文艺及自然等方面的认识，是琴棋书画四艺之一。国画和西方绘画有许多不同的地方：中国画重神韵，西方绘画重形似；中国画多用线条，西洋画线条都不显著；中国画不注重透视法，画作多以写云、山、树、瀑布等远望如天然平面物的东西，而西方绘画极注重透视法，力求画面上的物体跟真物一样；国画题材以自然为主，而西方绘画题材以人物为主。

参考答案

话题一　历史

课文 1　北京中轴线

1.（1）南北走向

（2）中轴突出（1 分）、两翼对称（1 分）

（3）3.7 公里

（4）紫禁城坐落于中轴线中心位置

2.（1）核心思想

（2）至高无上

（3）不可分割

（4）为人处世

（5）生机勃勃

3.（1）错。全长近 8 公里的中轴线

（2）错。“中”代表中心

（3）错。中轴线北端和南端为商业区

（4）错。中轴线见证了北京城的沧桑变迁

（5）对。北起奥林匹克公园

课文 2　大运河

1.（1）京杭大运河　（2）浙东运河　（3）天津市　（4）海河　（5）黄河

2.（1）大运河的开通打通了南北水上交通的大动脉

（2）成就了沿岸一个又一个富足的城市

（3）盐业、茶业、丝织业

3.（1）C　（2）A　（3）F　（4）G　（5）B

话题二　文化遗产

课文 1　三星堆文物

1.（1）E （2）A （3）C （4）B （5）G

2.（1）3000 至 5000 年的历史

（2）眼睛突出（1 分），两耳尖耸向两边张开（1 分）

（3）甲亢病

（4）（涮）火锅

3. A　D　E　F　H

课文 2　云冈石窟

1.（1）D （2）A （3）C （4）D （5）A

2.（1）C （2）F （3）B （4）A （5）D

3.（1）绵延 （2）经营 （3）纪录 （4）明显 （5）蔓延

话题三　发明

课文 1　傣族医药

1.A　B　F　G　H

2.（1）内服（1 分）和外用（1 分）

（2）因为西双版纳是中国热带生态系统保存最完整的地区。

（3）生物多样性

（4）可以增收致富

3.（1）C　（2）F　（3）A　（4）D　（5）B

课文 2　中国烟花

1.（1）对。在中国，以火药制作的烟花爆竹有着悠久的历史。

（2）错。多种形式的焰火表演与音乐交织

（3）对。特效焰火“人民万岁”

（4）错。均是高科技环保焰火产品

（5）对。早在 1000 多年前，中国古人从炼丹起火中认识并发明了火药。

2.（1）享有盛誉

（2）震撼人心

（3）枝繁叶茂

（4）俨然

（5）浪漫主义

3.（1）A　（2）C　（3）F　（4）B　（5）H

话题四　艺术

课文 1　京剧脸谱

1.B　C　D　G　H

2.（1）很强的装饰性（1 分）和形式美感（1 分）

（2）通天纹勾长“寿”字

（3）鼻梁突起（1 分），形象更加雄壮（1 分）。

3.（1）D　（2）A　（3）F　（4）C　（5）H

课文 2　剪纸——刀尖上的艺术

1.（1）C　（2）D　（3）D　（4）C　（5）C

2.（1）有千年之久

（2）纸的发明

（3）明清时期

（4）花、鸟、走兽、人、汉字（任选两个）

3.（1）C　（2）E　（3）A　（4）B　（5）G

出 版 人：王君校
策划编辑：张　超
责任编辑：杨　晗
英文编辑：薛彧威
封面设计：北京几何创想艺术设计有限公司
排　　版：北京颂煜文化传播有限公司
印刷监制：汪　洋

图书在版编目（CIP）数据

中国文化精读教程．传统文化 / 冯薇薇，张超编著．-- 北京：华语教学出版社，2025.4
ISBN 978-7-5138-2562-7

Ⅰ．①中… Ⅱ．①冯… ②张… Ⅲ．①汉语 - 对外汉语教学 - 教材 Ⅳ．① H195.4

中国国家版本馆 CIP 数据核字 (2024) 第 032855 号

中国文化精读教程·传统文化

冯薇薇　张超　编著

*

华语教学出版社有限责任公司出版
（中国北京百万庄大街 24 号　邮政编码 100037）
电话：(86)10-68320585, 68997826
传真：(86)10-68997826, 68326333
网址：www.sinolingua.com.cn
电子信箱：hyjx@sinolingua.com.cn
北京虎彩文化传播有限公司印刷
2025 年（16 开）第 1 版
2025 年第 1 版第 1 次印刷
ISBN 978-7-5138-2562-7
006900